This little book
belongs to

LIFE HAS NO BLESSING LIKE A GOOD FRIEND

All You Need Is a Friend

Illustrated by
Mary Engelbreit

**Andrews McMeel
Publishing**

Kansas City

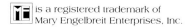 is a registered trademark of Mary Engelbreit Enterprises, Inc.

www.andrewsmcmeel.com

ISBN: 0-8362-0795-5

All You Need
Is a Friend

When a sunny hello
would help brighten your day ...

When you've just heard
good news and
have volumes to say ...

I Love to hear from you!

When two tickets
turn up to a great matinee ...

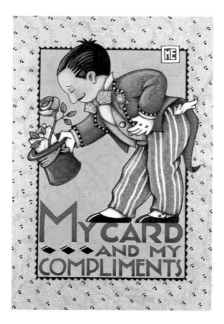

... all you need is a friend!

When the path that you're on
turns surprisingly rough ...

When wherever you're going,
the going gets tough ...

When you're giving your all
but it's just not enough ...

... all you need is a friend!

A friend speaks the truth
when it needs to be told ...

GOSSIP

Tells you you're radiant
when you feel old ...

WE ARE ALWAYS THE SAME AGE INSIDE.

Gives you a nudge
when you must be cajoled ...
likes you as you are ...

CLOUDS MAY COME, BUT CLOUDS MUST GO,
AND THEY HAVE A SILVER LINING,
FOR BEYOND THEM ALL, YOU KNOW,
THE SUN OR MOON IS SHINING.

Joins in your mischief
with vigor and zest ...

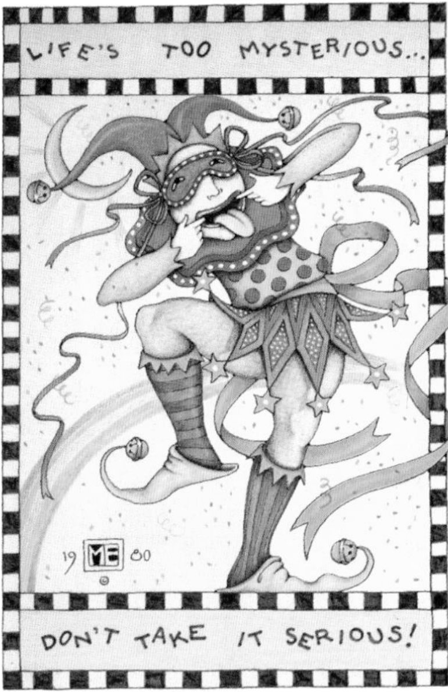
LIFE'S TOO MYSTERIOUS...
19 ME 80
©
DON'T TAKE IT SERIOUS!

Makes you aware that
you're looking your best ...

Leaves you alone
if you just need a rest ...
but never strays too far.

When a role model's needed
to keep you on track ...

When you've tried to be open
but don't have the knack ...

When you've earned a good word
and a pat on the back ...

... all you need is a friend.

FOR THERE IS NO FRIEND LIKE A SISTER IN CALM OR STORMY WEATHER

—CHRISTINA ROSSETTI

When it's shared, every day
can be even more fun ...

And a duo is often
much better than one ...

So remember each dawn
as you rise with the sun ...
all you need is a friend!

AH! HOW GOOD IT FEELS THE HAND of an OLD FRIEND

—LONGFELLOW

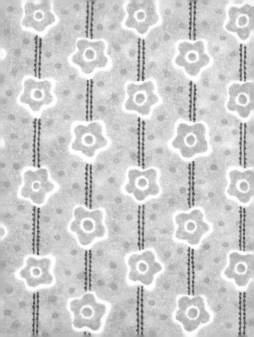